Setting and Achieving Goals

By George K. Wood

Table of Contents

Introduction

Researchers polled Yale's graduating seniors in 1953 to see how many of them had definite, documented aspirations for the future. The correct answer is 3%. Twenty years later, researchers questioned the Class of 1953 surviving members and discovered that the 3% with objectives had acquired more personal financial worth than the other 97% of the class combined!

This story's moral is:

1. Goals are effective.
2. They are hardly ever used.

I'm assuming you already want more out of life than you now have and are looking for a means to attain it. That's precisely what you'll discover here: a method to acquire it regardless of your history, age, or circumstances.

There are three sections in "How to Set and Achieve a Goal—Free Trial":

I. How to Make a Goal
II. How to Reach a Goal
III. Techniques for Motivation

Will "How to Set and Achieve a Goal" help me accomplish what I want out of life?" Absolutely!

"How to Set and Achieve a Goal" works if you use it. It truly teaches you how to make your desires come true, but only those ones that you are willing to make come true.

This book teaches you how to devote the time and effort required to achieving your goals in life. But you must put up the effort and devote the time.

Do not just read this book! Reading this book will not benefit you. Stick to the basic step-by-step approach! Take action now! Use strong tactics!

And I guarantee that all of your wishes will be granted.

Chapter 1

How to Make a Goal

How do you select a goal?

Do you have difficulty deciding on a goal? Do you have an excessive number? Or do you have no objectives at all? Then this is the chapter for you!

We all desire to live better lives. We all have dreams. Wishes are objectives, but they have a snap, crackle, and pop to them. Goals give you the procedure that will get you where you want to go, but all too frequently they do not, the impetus to get you there.

Wishes are unique. They have an effect similar to being hit by lightning rather than a lightning bug. They allow you to fantasize. They let you fly. They allow you to tap into a reservoir of endless possibilities and boundless vitality, giving you the ability to do things you could never have dreamed of before.

If you want to make things happen in your life, focus on making your wishes come true rather than setting objectives.

You must first select what you want before you can make your fantasies come true. Many individuals labor week after week, thinking of a nice life, but they seldom have a clear picture of what that "good life" should be.

Not what you're meant to want, not what others want for you, but what you truly desire for yourself.

1. Are you prepared to pay the price?

A famous pianist performed a performance at a cocktail party one evening. Her hostess stated afterwards, "I would give anything to be able to play like you."

"No, you wouldn't," the pianist said after a few minutes of contemplation." I most certainly would," the hostess answered, astonished and humiliated in front of her visitor, shaking her head. "You'd like to play as I do now, but you're not willing to."

To learn how to play that style, you must practice eight hours a day for twenty years.

Take anything you want, but pay for it, said God. - Proverb from Spain.

Every wish has a cost. If you're ready to pay the price, you can have everything you desire. The cost might be time, money, or effort. It might be in what you have to give up to acquiring what you desire.

Your willingness to pay the price is what gives you the authority to make your dream come true. You are 100% likely to succeed if you are 100% willing to pay the price.

Your request will be granted if you pay the cost.

Chapter 2

How to Reach a Goal

Step 1: Inspire Desire.

"Desire is the first and most important step in achieving one's goals."

Have you established personal or corporate objectives and failed to meet them?

Here's an important question: WHY?

The reason is simple: we did not have a strong enough desire.

Some may argue against this. "But I had a great desire, yet I still didn't get there." Sorry, but the desire was still insufficient.

How do you recognize tremendous desire and passion?

It's what keeps people working all hours, getting up early and going to bed late.

Conversation, thought, and action are all dominated by desire.

Consider the goals you've set for yourself for a minute. How dedicated are you to achieving these objectives?

Under what circumstances would you give up?

What if you could greatly boost your desire to attain these objectives?

What if you desired them so much that you knew with full confidence that you would never, ever give up?

When you are fully devoted to achieving your objectives, you shift from hoping to knowing. If you truly desire something, leaving is just not an option. You must either discover a method or create one. Whatever it takes, you pay the price.

You may fulfill an unachievable ideal by instilling tremendous desire.

Create a genuine desire to attain the goal. A desire or daydream is meaningless; it is hazy, unformed, and unsupported by action. Desire drives action in your strategy. A strong desire is a powerful force for achievement.

Chapter 3

Step 2 - Create Belief

If you don't think you can achieve a goal, it will remain a pipe dream just as much as if you don't bother preparing the path or doing what's necessary to get there.

If you have any doubts that you will be able to complete a task, you will not give it your best. In fact, you may simply put it away. To truly achieve something, you must first think it is possible at the cellular level.

Believing equals seeing. Believing comes from seeing.

We're convinced you'll attain your objectives if you're prepared to accept that you can be successful, that you'll like being successful, and if you're willing to build and work on a thrilling, fun, and gratifying road to success.

Step 3: Establish Your Goal.

In May 1961, John F. Kennedy declared that America would put a man on the moon "before the decade is up." It was a daring and audacious goal, maybe the greatest of all time.

However, simply stating the remark did not result in its fulfillment.

Putting a man on the moon requires enormous quantities of knowledge, study, planning, money, people, risk, and dedication, among other things. The most significant step, however, was not Neil Armstrong's but John F. Kennedy's establishment of the Objective.

The objective is the ultimate objective. It is the end result of all your efforts. For example, in investing, it may be to have $5 million by retirement.

While some individuals choose to have an objective in only one area of their lives, most successful people have objectives in several areas:

Retirement A Spiritual Career Family Financial Health Knowledge Material

These are only a few of the categories in which you should place your objectives. Long-term goals, perhaps even lifetime goals, are common, although they are not required. They must be meaningful to you and something you believe is worthwhile to pursue, or else having a goal-setting habit would be pointless.

To begin a goal-making habit, we recommend creating objectives in one or two categories. As you begin to achieve little accomplishments, you will most likely add additional objectives since you want to be successful in all aspects of your life.

Remember, don't be shy:

Make your goals as big as you can practically achieve them. Make sure your objectives are S.M.A.R.T.!!!

Commit to setting SMART objectives and begin working toward them right now.

Chapter 4

Write it Down

Write down your aim in great detail.

What is the significance of writing it down?

Words are an essential component of the cognitive process. Words create mental images, pictures, sensations, and emotions. By encasing it in words, abstract thinking gains embodiment, shape, form, and substance.

It is no longer simply an idea!

It becomes something that stimulates us or gives us a gut sensation.

What is the significance of the mechanical act of writing?

Continuing from where we left off, putting pen to paper now transforms those phrases that encapsulate ideas into something physical. We may now examine it physically.

Even the process of coordinating the eye with the hand holding the pen leaves a far stronger impact on our minds when we type down the word or statement.

When we read and re-read that word or statement, the impact on our minds grows stronger and stronger.

Written objectives are directions to the unconscious mind, which blindly obeys them. Writing out one's goals has a semi-magical effect that makes accomplishing well-written goals practically guaranteed. The true technique is to write down one's goals in a unique method that ensures their realization. Make a note of it or kiss it goodbye.

Chapter 5

Step 5 - Establish a Deadline

Set a deadline for achieving your objective. Setting a deadline for achieving your objective ignites the goal-seeking rocket in your imagination. Make sure your date is feasible. Not so soon that it becomes impossible, but not too late that it becomes uninteresting. Make a note of the date of your objective right next to it. You should never change this date after you've set it.

Can we understand why deadlines are another critical stage in goal achievement?

Yes, deadlines help to focus minds and boost motivation. It would be a mistake, however, to believe that deadlines accomplish miracles.

Setting a target and declaring, "In seven days, I will have made an extra $5,000" will not work unless you have a strategy and a realistic plan based on your current circumstances.

Make a deadline. Deadlines motivate us to take action.

When we don't add a date to our goal, when we commit to completing it "as soon as possible," the goal ends up in our "as soon as possible" pile of things I'll do another day, which is probably never. Why?

Because we all have too much to accomplish and not enough time to complete it all. Items with completion deadlines tend to rise in priority and importance, causing us to take action and complete them.

A thousand mile trip begins with a single step. No goal is achieved by leaping across a chasm. Many people are terrified and pushed away from pursuing what they truly desire in life for fear of having to take a gigantic leap across that chasm and, hey, what if I don't leap far enough? Disaster.

But until you write down your objective, define it, and set a deadline to break it down into manageable steps, it will always look like it is too far out of reach and hence impossible. However, if you follow these three stages and break down the objective, you will always find that you have control over what it takes to complete the next step. And once you get started, you're on your way! Step 6: Explain Your Motives

According to research on goal setting and the keys to success, many people fail to attain success simply because they lack clear reasons for doing so.

Don't let anything get in the way of your achievement. Consider why you desire to attain an objective, and then put down your decision.

Do you want to retire with $5 million? Why? You want to live in a mansion, right? Why? The more convincing your reasons are, the more likely you are to meet your objectives.

If you can't come up with "excellent" reasons, you might as well create another goal because this one won't be met.

Remember that everyone has their own reasons for desiring something. What one person considers vain or dumb, another considers valuable or amazing.

You must develop reasons that are honest, powerful, and compelling to you.

Write them down underneath the relevant objective, with plenty of room to develop or add to them. The more justification you have, the better. Just make sure they truly express your reasons for wanting something.

Chapter 6

Step 6: Establish Your SUB-GOALS

After you've developed an objective and persuasive reasons for accomplishing it, you must begin planning your path to the objective.

"What measures do I need to take to..."

These steps will serve as your sub-goals.

Assume you've established a goal of having $5 million by retirement (which may be 20 years or more away). First, you must choose how you will accomplish this. Do you want to know more about investing? Will you be required to start saving $500 every week? Do you have to look for a new job? Will you have to keep a closer eye on your existing investments? Whatever has to be done to move you closer to your objective will become your sub-goals.

Sub-goals might be narrow or extensive in scope, but they must always go directly to the objective they serve. They must also have a deadline at all times. A date by which you want to complete the sub-goal, preferably one that is both motivating and assures progress toward your objective,

Typically, you will have numerous sub-goals at once, and in the case of a true long-term objective, some of the sub-goals may be unclear at first, with others emerging when certain current sub-goals are met.

Always keep track of your sub-goals and their completion dates. You don't want to be overwhelmed by your sub-goals if they are too long or too challenging. If a sub-goal is long-term (for example, earning a four-year degree toward a bigger career objective), break it down into smaller portions (every year, for example), then modify and/or renew them when completed.

Making appropriate and realistic sub-goals and completing them on schedule can allow you to make significant progress toward objectives that may appear frightening, or even unachievable, on their own.

Chapter 7

Step 7: Plan Out Your Tasks

Just as we divide major or long-term objectives into smaller supporting aspects known as sub-goals, we divide our sub-goals into even smaller pieces. These minor components are

They are called tasks, and completing them is what makes goal setting truly effective. Sub-goals are often the easy tasks that must be completed in order to achieve a sub-goal.

If you've set a sub-goal, say, to have a thorough grasp of bond investing by next June 15th, you'll need to complete a lot of tasks to get there.

A task would be to go to the library and obtain a book about bonds.

Reading the book for one hour on Monday, Wednesday, and Friday might be divided into three independent tasks.

Another task would be to go to the Investors Skills website and look for bond information. It would also be a task to call a friend who has had success in the bond market.

All of these tasks, which should be written down on the same piece of paper as the sub-goal they support, must be assigned an Accomplishment Date, because if you procrastinate calling your buddy, never finish reading the book, or don't bother checking the website, you won't meet your sub-goal of learning about bonds by its Accomplishment Date.

And, sadly for you, this will turn your $5 million retirement goal into a pipe dream. It didn't have to be this way.

You'll make tremendous progress toward your sub-goals and objectives without feeling overwhelmed if you focus your concentration on easy-to-complete tasks and complete those tasks.

Make a list of ALL tasks, including ones that will only take a few minutes to accomplish. Then, once completed, cross them off your list.

As more tasks are successfully completed and marked off, you'll find yourself growing more encouraged and confident in your talents.

The more you believe, the harder you will work and the more you will love accomplishing additional tasks.

And the more tasks you finish on time, the closer you'll be to the success you truly desire. Your initial definition of success is your objective.

The First Step's Secret

Do you know the most crucial goal-setting secret? Yes? So, what are you holding out for?

Chapter 8

Techniques of Motivation

1. Success Enhancements in Action

What Exactly Are Success Enhancements?

There are two critical components to success.

The first is goal setting, which is simply: identifying objectives, developing compelling reasons for desiring the objectives, breaking the objectives down into manageable sub-goals, and breaking the sub-goals down into manageable tasks. The second critical component is to train your mind to think favorably.

You must cultivate an accomplishment attitude in order to attain your goals. While evaluating your reasons and checking off completed tasks are two things you should do to keep your mind focused on the success you want.

There are five more success enhancements we recommend you learn about: Success Questions, Success Stimulants, Visualization Techniques, and Affirmations

1. Reward Methodology

When you can keep your mind focused on achieving an achievement, you will almost certainly achieve it.

2. Visualization Method

The brain frequently thinks in terms of images.

With a single glance, the human eye gathers an enormous quantity of information and conveys it to the brain, which then converts that information into the form we 'see.'

It is more accurate to say that we see with our brains rather than our eyes. The success strategy I'm referring to is visualizing. I assure you that "visualizing your results is the key to attaining your outcomes

Visualization is one of the most essential skills you will ever master, and it is used by all strong achievers.

One of the reasons goal planning fails for individuals is that they don't grasp or leverage the power of this one crucial component. You may set a goal, write it down, and even read it aloud every day, but if you can't visualize yourself in possession of it, you'll never achieve it long term.

Visualization is essential to your success for two reasons:

1. Your mind thinks in terms of visuals and images.
2. Your conduct is dictated by your subconscious mind.

When you hammer something into your mind in great detail, it becomes a part of your reality.

Your subconscious mind cannot tell the difference between what is genuine and what is vividly imagined. Whatever image (objective) you have in mind will drive your activities to generate that precise image.

When you envision yourself in possession of your objective on a regular basis, your subconscious mind will direct you to activities that correspond to the mental image you have.

3. Affirmation Method

Affirmations are statements we make to ourselves. They are verbal suggestions that we make either silently or aloud.

The reality is that if you repeat something to yourself enough times, you will ultimately believe it.

Affirmations, often known as self-talk, are a fairly popular pastime.

"Things like this happen to me all the time!"

"I just can't seem to lose weight!"

"I'm such a clumsy person!"

" Is this anything you've heard before?

But we may also affirm our own strengths. We can even confirm abilities that we do not yet possess.

Create daily affirmations that reinforce the goals you established during goal setting. You must determine what changes you must make in yourself to make it simpler to practice or keep the commitments you made in your goal setting.

Conclusion

In conclusion, wishes are objectives, but they have a snap, crackle, and pop to them. Goals give you the procedure that will get you where you want to go, but all too frequently they do not, the impetus to get you there. You must first select what you want before you can make fantasies come true. Desire is the first and most important step in achieving one's goals. Create a genuine desire to attain the goal.

Believing comes from seeing. If you don't think you can achieve a goal, it will remain a pipe dream just as much as if you do not bother preparing the path. John F. Kennedy declared that America would put a man on the moon "before the decade is up". Most successful people have objectives in several areas. Long-term goals, perhaps even lifetime goals, are common.

They must be meaningful to you and something you believe is worthwhile to pursue. Establish a deadline for achieving your objective. Deadlines motivate us to take action and make items with completion deadlines more important. Writing out one's goals has a semi-magical effect that makes accomplishing well-written goals practically guaranteed. Make a note of the date of your objective right next to it.

Many people fail to attain success simply because they lack clear reasons for doing so. If you can't come up with "excellent" reasons for accomplishing an objective, you might as well create another goal. Step 6: Establish your sub-goals and plan your path to the objective. Making appropriate and realistic sub-goals and completing them on schedule can allow you to make significant progress toward objectives that may appear frightening, or unachievable, on their own. Step 7: Plan Out Your Sub-Goals and Assign an Accomplishment Date.

Make a list of ALL tasks, including ones that will only take a few minutes to accomplish. Then, once completed, cross them off your list. If you can't visualize yourself in possession of an objective, you'll never achieve it. Affirmations are verbal suggestions that we make to ourselves silently or aloud. Create daily affirmations that reinforce the goals you established during goal-setting.

www.ingramcontent.com/pod-product-compliance
Lightning Source LLC
La Vergne TN
LVHW020534160826
845677LV00015B/4057
* 9 7 9 8 3 5 7 3 1 0 8 5 9 *